George Rainsford Fairbanks

Florida

Its history and its romance

George Rainsford Fairbanks

Florida
Its history and its romance

ISBN/EAN: 9783337037765

Printed in Europe, USA, Canada, Australia, Japan

Cover: Foto ©ninafisch / pixelio.de

More available books at **www.hansebooks.com**

GREATER
SACRAMENTO

HER ACHIEVEMENTS RESOURCES AND POSSIBILITIES

KELMAN & COMPANY

PVBLISHERS—919 Sixth Street—SACRAMENTO

Photographs by McCurry Photo Company
Engravings by Sutter Photo Engraving Company
Printed by the H. S. Crocker Company
Paper from Richardson-Case Paper Company

CALIFORNIA STATE CAPITOL

SACRAMENTO'S FUTURE

BY D.W. CARMICHAEL
PRES. SACRAMENTO CHAMBER OF COMMERCE

CALIFORNIA, the name of which, s nce the days of forty-nine, has been sweet music to the ear of the civilized world; California, from whose mines untold millions of wealth has been taken; California whose forests are vast and primeval; California, with her wonderful oil production, affording to-day, the cheapest fuel to the manufacturer of any state in the Union; California, though a new state, as she is to-day, stands as a leader in agriculture and horticulture; California, whose Western shore is washed by the Pacific Ocean for nine hundred miles, and from which the cool breezes temper the atmosphere of the summer evening in every hamlet of this great state, and makes living here worth while.

Located in such a state is the great Sacramento Valley; a Valley whose area excels that of the whole State of Massachusetts; a Valley which has for its head, the glistening snow-capped peaks of the monarch of all mountains, Mt. Shasta; a Valley which can rightfully be spoken of as the garden of the world, through which run the sinuous sparkling streams, watering the potent soil and bringing forth every manner of fruit, flower and tree, known to north and south, east and west; a Valley

FORT SUTTER, CALIFORNIA'S HISTORIC LANDMARK
Erected 1839

VIEW OF SACRAMENTO FROM THE DOME OF STATE CAPITOL
LOOKING NORTHWEST

with five million acres of the most fertile soil in the world, surrounded by mountains of perpetual snow, and from the foot of which springs forth that wonderful waterway, the Sacramento River, the fifth river in agricultural importance in the whole United States, watering this great Valley from end to end, and upon whose bosom, boats laden with every product of farm, garden, mill and mine, go back and forth between San Francisco and Red Bluff, a distance of 300 miles.

Think of it! A navigable river winding through millions of fertile acres for more than 300 miles, and not only does this magnificent stream afford irrigation and shipping transportation, but as a source of food supply, it is unsurpassed. Millions of pounds of fish are taken from this river for shipment abroad as well as home consumption.

I say to the mechanic and miner, the agriculturalist and the laborer, that from Mt. Shasta to Sacramento, and from Vacaville to Newcastle, there is work and wealth beyond your fondest dream.

To the banker and lawyer, merchant and professional man, here is a section whose possibilities for commercial development is unsurpassed.

To the manufacturer, the resources of this Valley are beyond cavil, the grandest of any section in the United States to-day. The multiplicity of raw material, cheap transportation, the unlimited electric power that can be developed, are advantages for manufacturers that cannot remain unnoticed by the great manufacturers of this country.

To the tourists, no section of the Great West contains more interest from both scenic and historical standpoint, than does this great Valley. It was here that the pioneers of early days

first came into the Golden West. It was here, in the foothills of this great Valley, that gold was discovered, the lure that brought thousands of treasure-seeking souls from all ends of the earth.

This Valley offers to those in search of health, our pineclad hills and our matchless climate, with many mineral and medicinal springs, which rival those of Southern Europe.

It is here in this beautiful Valley that the artist will be inspired by the blue skies and purple and white mountain ranges, and the towering peaks of everlasting snow, and mirroring waters of lake and stream.

In this Valley the writer's inspiration will come from quaint homes, blooming orchards and fertile fields.

This is my faint picture of the surrounding country of Sacramento City. Sacramento, the capital of this great State that I have spoken of; Sacramento, the hub of this great Valley I have spoken of; Sacramento, the home city of 65,000 happy souls, a city whose population and wealth have both doubled in the past six years; a city whose future cannot be pictured and scarcely imagined, a city which in your time and mine will become one of the greatest inland cities in these United States; a city which ten years from to-day will be unloading cargoes from European countries at the foot of our streets from laden boats on the Sacramento River.

NEW CITY HALL

GREATER SACRAMENTO

BY S. GLEN ANDRUS

OPPORTUNITY knocks at the door of cities, as it does at the door of the individual, and fortunate, indeed, is the city whose civic pride and activity is such that opportunity turns not away in discouragement. Sacramento is a splendid example of a city that is making the most of its opportunity, and there is no city on the Pacific Coast, today, at which the finger of opportunity is beckoning with such insistency as to the Capital City of California.

The statement cannot be successfully challenged that the whilom, typical, somnolent Capital City of the most gloriously endowed state in the Union, is, to-day, the center of the greatest development on the Pacific Coast. Neither can the statement be successfully denied that no city in the world has, or ever did have, such an agricultural empire as that of which Greater Sacramento is the mistress and also the logical, distributing center.

Still one other statement can be made that is equally incapable of successful denial, to the effect that, never in the history of the Pacific Coast, was there greater opportunity offered for the homeseeker and the investor than is offered, to-day, in Sacramento City, Sacramento County and Sacramento Valley. There are many sound reasons for these tremendous facts, for to no other city in the United States, at least, have so many great commercial and industrial changes come in so short a period. The greatest of these was the breaking up of the enormous grain ranches, which,

THE ELKS' RECEPTION ROOM

ELKS' BUILDING

for years, made California the largest grain-producing state in the Union. Until the greatest granary the world has ever produced was ruined by wanton husbandry, Sacramento was starving for agricultural development, the basis of all large commercial centers.

Upon the colossal ruin of that granary is now being builded an agricultural empire of intensive farming, largely under irrigation, and it is an empire of more than 3,000,000 acres of fertile valley land, and almost an equal amount of foothill land on which both citrus and deciduous fruits flourish. Owing to the fortunate geographical location of Sacramento, and to the mountain ranges on either side of the Valley, this city must be the outlet of the almost undreamed of agricultural and mineral production of the future. In the mute language of every large city in the United States, these facts mean a population of, at least, a half million people for Greater Sacramento before this empire shall have been fully developed.

Of Sacramento, Frank A. Vanderlip, president of the City National Bank of New York, and one of the most powerful financial men of the nation, said: "I could not be as modest as you men of Sacramento seem to be, were I a citizen of a city possessing a partially developed agricultural empire of 6,000,000 acres of fertile soil, an empire traversed by rivers of wonderful possibilities."

That he was not dealing in flattery, was shown by the fact that he and his friends afterwards invested more than $2,000,000 in the lands of the agricultural empire which had so astonished him. Think of it! Wall Street money pouring into land investments in the Sacramento Valley, 3,000 miles distant; Wall Street money, which hitherto shriveled when anything was mentioned that did not savor of the known certainty, as of death or taxes.

In this agricultural empire is to be found the keynote to Sacramento's future. The National government is recognizing the greatness of the city's future by entertaining a report by engineers recommending the expenditure of $33,000,000 for the purpose of controlling the flood waters of the Sacramento and San Joaquin Rivers, which, among other things, will permit of the reclamation of over 1,000,000 acres of river-bottom land as rich as the delta of the Nile. Governmental recognition is also given in the approval of a project for a nine-foot channel from the delta of the river to Sacramento, and in the appropriation of $400,000 to "uncork" the river at its mouth; and, still further, in doubling the appropriation for keeping navigation open the year round as far north as Red Bluff, 300 miles from the delta.

That Sacramentans are alive to the future of the city and are acquiring a wholesome Sacramento spirit, is shown by the accomplished fact of "Greater Sacramento," which has a population of fully 65,000.

With its seven banks, totaling over $24,000,000 in deposits, and showing approximately $79,000,000 clearings for the year 1911; with its new high school; new city hall; new court house; six new, modern hotels; nearly a score new, modern, class A office buildings; with building operations totaling fully $9,000,000; with its more than forty miles of paved streets; with its 100 miles of oil-macadam roads leading into productive territory in the county; with two transcontinental lines of railroad; two interurban lines, and several others projected, and with the indomitable spirit that has been awakened and illustrated by the raising of over $190,000 for a new Y. M. C. A. building, the future of Greater Sacramento cannot fail to be a brilliant one.

PEOPLES SAVINGS BANK BUILDING

SACRAMENTO AS THE FINANCIAL CENTER OF THE SACRAMENTO VALLEY

BY ALDEN ANDERSON

THE banks of a community bear the same relation to its industrial and commercial life as the heart does to the human system. Money is the industrial life blood, and going through the arteries of trade is essential, in this day of intricate and extensive exchange of commodities, to the continued existence of our present-day standard of living.

Banks are the financial warehouses, and, therefore, for the purpose of this article, I will consider the assets of the banks as the financial barometer. It is not my intention to relate past history of banking in Sacramento. A comparison of the total assets of the banks of Sacramento of 1890-1900 and the present time will suffice to show the growth and increase of the financial power of the city.

There is, quite generally, much confusion in the minds of those who do not give the matter deep thought or study, as to the function of banks and the source from whence the bulk of the assets of the banks come. Banks do not coin money or create wealth. Rather do they reflect the status, the condition and the resources of the place or district wherein they are located. They are the conservators or concentrators of the values made by others, and, if a community has no value there would be no banks, or need of them, to handle their finances.

The total assets of the banks in Sacramento in 1890, were $8,255,897.60; in 1900, $10,754,010.35, and, at the present time, $35,487,717.88. This is a splendid record, for the banks of this city are noted for their substantiality and for their solidity and conservativeness.

INTERIOR VIEW OF CAPITAL NATIONAL BANK

NEW HOME OF NATIONAL BANK OF D. O. MILLS & CO.

With the above as a criterion, it needs no argument to prove the importance of Sacramento as a financial center. A broad valley surrounding it on all sides with soil as prolific as the famed Valley of the Nile, but with a far greater variety of production. Beyond, the hills, with their thousands of acres of pasture, and the mountains with their forests of timber and deposits of mineral wealth, with water transportation to the sea, and the main lines of railroads leading north and south, east and west, there is no single necessary element lacking to prevent a continual increase of wealth, of development and social and material progress.

The development of this rich country has not much more than attained a good headway as yet, but the signs of the times indicate a rapid increase and every step forward will add to the potency and power of Sacramento as a financial center. A bank, if properly conducted, cannot legally, and should not from caution, "back" any industrial, commercial or agricultural enterprise. As they accumulate money, representing values created by others, and have funds to loan, they do so to those with established credit, or on approved security. As the community grows and more values are created, more and more people have established credit, or are in a position to give the necessary security to obtain the loanable funds of the banks. With the funds thus secured factories are established, lands are brought under cultivation, mines exploited and the general forward movement goes on.

In a country so rich in natural resources, and many of them of such enormous extent, it is absolutely necessary to obtain "outside" capital to assist or make possible the earliest development.

CALIFORNIA NATIONAL BANK—HOME OF THE SUTTER CLUB

As the smaller places in the Valley look to Sacramento, so does Sacramento look to other places. If the undertaking is too large for the available capital here to undertake, San Francisco, as the next nearer and larger center, would be appealed to. If San Francisco has something too large for their available capital, Chicago, New York, or other large and potent financial centers would be called upon, and, thus the movement goes on, each center acting within the scope of its own possibilities. But once the enterprise is under way, the values created stay and assist in the general upbuilding.

There is a splendid balancing of things that produce, create and make values, in the great Sacramento Valley. If one variety of fruit does not do well one season, another variety does. If the mines are quiet, the lumber men are active. If the sheep raisers are complaining of inactivity and poor prices the chances are the cattle men are thriving and prosperous, and so on down the line with hops, wines, olives, dried fruits, dairying, grain and the rest of our almost innumerable productions of the soil, always adding the increasing output of our factories and the enormous generation of electrical energy.

Thus it is, that the City of Sacramento, in the center of all this natural wonderland of richness and opportunity, serves, and will continue to serve, the different industries, as the accumulator and conservator of their values, as represented in money, and will go forward and onward to the same extent and in the same proportion as its industries prosper, its environs grow and as the people thrive.

That we will go forward there is no question. Our location, and environment assure us of continued growth and of a splendid and magnificent future.

JOHN BREUNER FURNITURE COMPANY, SACRAMENTO, ESTABLISHED IN 1856

HOW SACRAMENTO PROTECTS HER MANUFACTURERS AND MERCHANTS

BY C. MEREDITH

THE modern way of regarding a city as a business enterprise, in which each citizen is interested to a greater of less extent, has resulted in various organizations that specialize, each along different lines, but all toward the definite end of civic betterment. Better residential conditions for the working-man, better schools and more breathing spots in factory districts, more children's play grounds; these are part of the benefits that accrue to the humblest wage earner with civic advancement, while the man whose property interests are extensive, finds his returns measured up in dollars and cents.

But one thing, co-operation, is needed to bring about the maximum amount of accomplishment in city building, and not only should this co-operation include the various semi-public bodies, but also the different social clubs and neighborhood organizations, no matter for what purpose they exist. With this theory of co-operation as the foundation upon which it has built itself into public respect and confidence, in the remarkably short space of one year, the Sacramento Valley Home Products League affords the manufacturer, already established in the Sacramento Valley, its support, when the quality of his production and its price entitle him thereto, and, as an inducement to bring other manufacturers here, it assures them the support of a public educated in the knowledge that no better plan of city building can be evoked than that embodied in the home industry idea.

Acting upon the theory that the home merchant and manufacturer is entitled to the patronage of his friends and neighbors, the League has waged a consistent and continued educational cam-

FARMERS AND MECHANICS SAVINGS BANK   SACRAMENTO SAVINGS BANK

MODERN PLANT OF THE CONSUMERS ICE AND
COLD STORAGE CO.

VIEW OF CALIFORNIA WINERY, ONE OF
SACRAMENTO'S WINERIES

paign.   It has regarded no individual, but stood back of each industry with the sole idea of creating such additional consumption as would necessitate the employment of additional men in production, and, in so doing, it has worked toward co-operation, believing that no single organization, no matter how broad or laudable its scope, could accomplish the results to be achieved through the consolidated efforts of different bodies having separate aims and purposes, but all animated by a proper and unselfish spirit of civic pride.

To accomplish results the League has made its hardest fight against that tradition which has caused many firms and individuals to send their patronage away to some other and competing place, instead of keeping it at home and employing it in building toward a greater city.   It has, however, found no active opposition in its work; its theories are too soundly based to admit of argument, but, at the first, it fronted apathy, a frame of mind that was willing to track the well worn rut and let well enough alone.   The only cure for such a frame of mind is education, and along educational lines the League instituted a consistent campaign, preaching its propaganda on the highways and in the byways, through individual enthusiasts, and proclaiming them broadcast by the wizardry of printers' ink, always and ever declaring that it did not father a sentimental movement, but was working along purely practical lines, with but one object, the building of a manufacturing city, in view.

As a result of the League's work of the past twelve months, the manufacturer, who sees in Sacramento or the Sacramento Valley, a field for the employment of his capital, can safely consider, when measuring up the various elements that are offered as inducements, a public sentiment which has come to know that it is good business policy to help support local institutions as opposed to

outside ones, and that realizes the increased value of every man who finds a job open for him and begins productive work.

The approaching Panama-Pacific International Exposition will bring thousands and thousands of people into the Sacramento Valley, many of whom will undoubtedly make it their home. With this increased population there will come a greater demand for manufactured products of various kinds, and this demand will, naturally, seek the nearest large city. Sacramento combines every element necessary to the building of a manufacturing city, and will, inevitably, become a great and important one.

Working slowly, but surely, the Sacramento Valley Home Products League considers its greatest asset the confidence of the public which it has already achieved. With this confidence as a basis, the League is preparing to reach out, to continue its educational campaign along broader lines than it is at present working upon, with the purpose of proving to the residents of the Sacramento Valley that they owe Sacramento the duty of supporting its merchants and manufacturers, not merely from a sentimental point of view, but also because good business policy dictates such a course. The natural result will be not only to build up the city of Sacramento, but also to make the Valley a richer and more prosperous place. With this plan carried out to its logical conclusion Sacramento will have much to offer the manufacturer, and to him the League extends the assurance, that, should he see fit to locate here, he will find a people, firm in the knowledge that more can be accomplished in city building by adherence to the Home industry idea than by any other means, and ready to get behind and help consume the goods which he puts forth.

CARS OF THE NORTHERN ELECTRIC RAILWAY, NEARING SACRAMENTO

DEPOT OF THE WESTERN PACIFIC RAILROAD, THE NEW TRANSCONTINENTAL LINE

DEPOT AND SECTION OF YARDS OF THE SOUTHERN PACIFIC RAILROAD

SACRAMENTO HOTELS & TRANSPORTATION FACILITIES

⚜ BY H.THORP ⚜

 **E**VERY movement toward reform in this country sweeps the American continent like a great cyclone, whether it be prohibition reform, suffragette agitation, anti-trust movement, or the fashionable seasonable fads of our men and women. One cannot be in sympathy or agree with all these passing fancies, but I do think the present great wave of highway reformation now sweeping the land, will receive the endorsement and approval of every thoughtful, well-meaning man and woman.

It has taken ten years of persistent effort on the part of ourselves, but more particularly those of New York, New Jersey, Connecticut, and other Eastern States, to awaken from the lethargy and chains which bound us politically, and otherwise, holding back all improvement of our highways and byways, and consequently retarding the progress which finally came to the Eastern States, and is now coming to the great State of California. Every dollar properly invested in the construction of good roads will yield immediate return to the country through which it runs, far in excess of the dim expectancy of the average citizen.

All large cities are the result of concentrated business, their size and population being dependent on the wealth and natural resources of the adjacent territory, but not, of course, overlooking the absolute necessity of quick and easy transportation.

No city can ever hope to be thriving and prosperous without the necessary transportation facilities. The United States furnishes sufficient proof of this, when we look at such cities as New

COUNTY COURT HOUSE, SACRAMENTO

R. A. Herold, Architect

HOTEL SACRAMENTO. ONE OF THE MOST MAGNIFICENT HOSTELRIES ON THE COAST.

York, Chicago, St. Louis, New Orleans and San Francisco. All the direct result of their magnificent waterways and endless chain of railroads, through and over which the products of our country must pass, and the wealth of other nations pour in. The location of these cities and the advantages derived by their splendid transportation facilities completely annihilates competition and gives them a first place for all time.

While all cities cannot be great, certain localities have natural advantages. Perhaps no city in the state has more undeveloped natural advantages than Sacramento. It rests peacefully on the banks of the fifth greatest river in America. It has two great transcontinental railroads contributing to its greatness. It is a natural jobbing center for a valley rich beyond measure in agriculture and horticulture, all creating and fostering a phenomenal commerce and making it the banking headquarters of a marvelously rich and prosperous section of the country.

Take these things away and imagine conditions with railroads gone, waterways allowed to fill up, and magnificent boulevards permitted to crumble and decay. It would unavoidably mean destruction and annihilation. Hence, the only conclusion is, that these are the foundations upon which our city rests, Protect them, assist them, don't block them, and we cannot fail to have a city of 100,000 in the very near future. A little effort upon the part of the inhabitants is all that is necessary to insure this wonderful growth.

Then, let us remember, that three things are necessary and important; namely, rapid and cheap transportation, reaching out in every direction, navigable rivers, properly protected and cared for, and last, but not least, good hotels for the traveler. Where these three agencies exist we always find great and growing cities, concentrated business activity, and places of large commercial importance.

Sacramento has within its reach and tributary to it, a great region rich in forests, rivers, mines and wonderful agricultural possibilities. It must be in close touch with this large territory and make the people residing there its neighbors in every sense of the word. To do this we must encourage the building of railroads and interurban lines to establish closer relations, so that those desiring to sell the products of the soil, or intending to make purchases of any kind, are compelled to think, first and foremost, of Sacramento.

What has made Sacramento grow so rapidly during the past few years? During the long period of dormant inactivity we had everything we have now. All our undeveloped resources were available during the past fifty years. Our mountains, rivers and agricultural possibilities were just as much in evidence then as now. The question is quickly and easily answered by remembering the most important things which contributed toward this awakening.

1st—The coming of another great transcontinental road.
2nd—The building and projecting of an endless chain of electric railways.
3rd—The financing and building of a magnificent new hotel.

Enough has already been said about the necessity and importance of transportation, but little or nothing on the very vital question of good hotels. Poor hotels in a community are the worst advertisement any place can have. To have it known the length and breadth of the land, that you cannot accommodate the traveler, the tourist and the visitor, is simply to drive them away. The traveling public demand good hotels in every city placed upon its itinerary, and if it becomes known (and it cannot be concealed) that your hotels are poor, below the standard, and not provided with modern equipment and good service, that city is scratched off the list.

That Sacramento ranks well with other growing cities is evident from the several new hotels constructed the past few years. The new "Hotel Sacramento" is among the most luxurious in California. When Alden Anderson was made President of the Sacramento Hotel Company, this new hotel was made possible.

ROCK CRUSHING PLANT OF NATOMAS CONSOLIDATED, FAIR OAKS. LARGE QUANTITIES OF CRUSHED ROCK MAKE SACRAMENTO ROADS AMONG THE BEST IN THE STATE

ALFALFA FIELD IN NATOMAS RECLAMATION DISTRICT

The SACRAMENTO ~ VALLEY ~

BY O. H. MILLER

THE Sacramento Valley of California is a region of varied resources and industries. Agriculture is by far the most important industry, and the agricultural products greatly exceed, in value, those of any other natural resources. The products of the soil, lumber, stock and structural materials, last year, amounted to approximately $150,000,000 in the twelve counties which are considered as comprising the Sacramento Valley. This may not seem so very large when regarded as an annual crop value, but when one stops to think that it represents an income of $410,958 for every day in the year its importance is more easily appreciated. These figures for the Sacramento Valley seem all the more remarkable when it is fully understood that the value of her soil products can be increased many fold.

All of the Pacific Coast country is still young as compared with the Atlantic Coast and European countries. Sixty-five years is a short time in the life of any country or any people. And yet, in this short space the Sacramento Valley has grown from a grass covered prairie to a position of distinction. It has passed through the different stages of development which began with the discovery of gold at Coloma, followed by the parceling out of land in immense estates under the Mexican rule, the time of the cattle king, the period of supremacy in grain production, and up to the present day of "a small farm well tilled," or "The Land of the Small Homestead." The transition through these periods was rapid, although each is distinctly marked; and, notwithstanding the fact that all of the industries represented by these intervals are still here and annually turn many millions into the pockets of our people.

CARS OF THE CENTRAL CALIFORNIA TRACTION CO., ONE OF SACRAMENTO'S NEW SUBURBAN ELECTRIC ROADS

The Sacramento Valley was originally an inland sea, but centuries of washing from the mountains on either side have filled in the arm of the ocean with rich detritus in much the same manner as the Nile Valley was built up. On the west, the Coast Range Mountains, and on the east, the Sierra Nevadas pierce the sky line with peaks that never put off their mantles of snow. Splendid forests of pine, fir, spruce and cedar, by holding back the winter rains, vie with the eternal snows in giving the foothills and valley a water supply of rare quality and absolute certainty.

If anyone has been misled into believing that the "days of old, the days of gold, and the days of '49" have passed in California let him correct that impression. California now leads all other states in the production of gold. Even now, she turns into the coffers of the country more than $30,000,000 worth of the precious metal each year. Nearly all of this comes from the Sacramento Valley counties—their contribution over and beyond five times that amount of agricultural products.

Then, there is a "world" of light and power. Electricity is the modern force, and we have an abundance and some to spare to our neighbors. The precipitous mountains and many rivers and streams form the basis of an electric power development not equalled anywhere else in the known world. One celebrated authority said that it is possible to develop, in the mountains adjacent to the Sacramento Valley, as much electricity as there is now in use in the whole United States.

TYPICAL CALIFORNIA BUNGALOW, AMID ORANGE GROVES. HOME OF MRS. O. W. RUGGLES, FAIR OAKS.

I hesitate to look into the future and endeavor to fathom events that are yet to come, but I clearly see that this Valley is very soon to feel the vitalizing effects of the application of electrical energy to the myriad tasks of human industry. We now have it in the factories, electric railroads, shops and cities, but I feel that the time is not far away when it will be on the farm and will be the universal moving force in the field as well as in the centers of population. When that time comes it will certainly revolutionize the tilling of the soil, not only in the doing of the work, but in the transportation of the people and products, and in the social life of the community.

The people of the Pacific Coast are expecting much from the Panama Canal. The largest trans-Atlantic steamship companies are, it is stated, already making plans to send their largest vessels through the canal to San Francisco. This will give us rapid and cheap transportation for all of our products to the Atlantic seaboard and European countries. There will, undoubtedly, be a great saving in freight rates as a result of ocean competition through the canal. We are confident that, with the completion of the canal, will come a commerce that, under present conditions, is impossible. San Francisco, with the finest harbor on the globe, will be on the main highway of the world's commerce. The Sacramento Valley, at the very door of this highway, will certainly feel more forcibly than any other producing and exporting section of the world, the results of this commerce.

The vine industry, consisting of wine, table and raisin grapes, represents one of the greatest and most important of California's many soil products. At least seventy-five per cent of the entire grape output of the United States can be credited to the Golden State. Practically all of the raisins and grape brandies produced in this country come from California.

The grape, raisin and wine industry of this state represents an investment in excess of $100,-000,000, and gives employment to more than 60,000 persons. Of wine grapes, there is a total of 153,000 acres, of raisin grapes 86,000 acres, and of table grapes 30,000 acres, or a grand total of 269,000 acres devoted to the growing of grapes. This, in the aggregate, represents an industry in which this state takes a big lead. The Sacramento Valley has its portion of this splendid business.

There can be no question regarding the stability of the progress now under way. Its foundation is sunk deep in a diversity of natural resources not found in any other land. Its framework consists of an agriculture that is unique in the quantity and quality of crops. A progressive people are conserving and developing these resources and products to the utmost and are also inviting others to come and share them.

SOURCE OF WATER SUPPLY FOR FAIR OAKS AND VICINITY. DAM OF THE CALIFORNIA CORPORATION

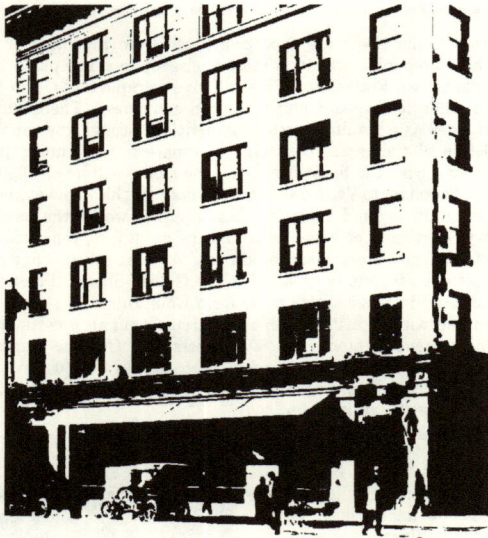

SUTTER NATIONAL BANK

SACRAMENTO
AS A FRUIT DISTRIBUTING CENTER
BY F. B. McKEVITT

SACRAMENTO is the logical and natural distributing point for the eastern shipments of California's deciduous fruits. This is true, not only because of the location of the city on the main line of the great railway that carries the larger portion of the crop, but especially because this city offers the natural outlet for the great Sacramento Valley on the north, and the wonderfully productive San Joaquin Valley on the south, these two contributing practically eighty per cent of the entire deciduous fruit output of the state.

Sacramento has fine railway facilities now, and they are constantly improving. Located upon the east bank of the Sacramento River, she has all the advantages of water transportation and the low rates that always follow such a location.

The city may be said to be the center of a network of railways. The main line of the Southern Pacific, which was the first transcontinental road to be built, has always enjoyed, and until within the last two years, has had a practical monopoly of transcontinental fresh fruit transportation. Two years ago the Western Pacific, a new transcontinental road, threw its lines open to business, and since that time has been a considerable factor in this business. In addition to these two great roads are several electric lines. The Northern Electric, which taps the rich country to the north of us as far as Chico and Oroville. To the south, the Central California Traction, an electric road, which

SACRAMENTO RIVER WATERFRONT, SHOWING SPLENDID SHIPPING FACILITIES

operates as far south as Stockton. Another line now in process of construction in the San Joaquin Valley, will tap very rich and productive sections, and, ultimately, exchange business with the Traction Line at Stockton, thus opening up to this city a territory which has not heretofore been tributary to Sacramento. To the west, the Vallejo & Northern, an electric line affiliated with the Northern Electric, is now building. This will provide access to the great fruit belt of Solano and Yolo, and, when the road is completed to Vallejo, connection will there be made with the Napa Valley electric line, opening up another large and rich territory. The Sacramento Southern Railway, following the course of the Sacramento River, in connection with the numerous transportation lines running boats upon the river, brings into the city the products of that wonderfully fertile section.

The Southern Pacific Railway has, for many years, given most careful and painstaking care to the transportation of fruit, and, since this railway has taken the business of refrigeration out of the hands of private companies, and performed this service in connection with the freight haul, great improvements have been inaugurated, until to-day it is beyond question that California enjoys the best transportation facilities of any fruit growing state in the world. The same fine refrigerator car service is also offered by the Western Pacific, which uses the same equipment as the Southern Pacific. All shipments routed over the Western are concentrated in Sacramento and delivered to the new line, which has made an enviable record in the expeditious and correct handling of this perishable product.

California's interstate shipments of fresh fruit in 1911, up to and including November 25th, excluding fractions of carloads, amount to

216 cars	Cherries
214 cars	Apricots
2,027 cars	Peaches
1,366 cars	Plums
2,324 cars	Pears
6,347 cars	Grapes
16 cars	Assorted Fruits

making a total of 12,512 cars of thirteen tons each, which equals 162,656 tons, or, practi-

cally, twelve million packages. It may be fairly estimated that the selling value of these shipments was about $12,000,000.00, of which one-half, or $6,000,000.00, represents the return to growers after all transportation and selling expenses have been deducted. This amount would have been much greater, but for the fact, that, after August 15th, California fruits were called upon to meet unusually heavy competition from eastern fruit crops, which, from that date until October 1st, were flooding all markets.

The greatest pear-producing section of the state is the rich Sacramento River district. The great table grape section is the northern part of the San Joaquin Valley. Vacaville, Winters and Suisun ship about 2,000 carloads of assorted fruits. The American River district nearly 1,000. Not less than 5,000 cars of grapes are shipped from the territory within forty miles of this city. The great bulk of our pears is grown within the same radius. Great tracts of land, which for years, produced nothing but hay, wheat or barley, with, perhaps, several thousand acres supporting less than half a dozen families, have passed out of the hands of their former owners and into the possession of more progressive and farseeing men. Water, for irrigation, has been brought in and distributed over large areas, which have been sub-divided into small tracts of ten and twenty acres, or more, and are now being sold to actual settlers. This land will be planted to fruits and alfalfa, to which it is specially adapted, and, in a few short years, will be supporting a large population, bringing prosperity to them and to the whole state. In this prosperity, Sacramento is sure to share in a greater measure than any other, as she is the nearest large city. Great reclamation projects are progressing to the north and west of us. Thousands of acres of overflowed lands will be rescued from the water and turned into fields, gardens and orchards of fertility unsurpassed, ready to direct their streams of golden reward into our channels of trade, further to upbuild and strengthen the beautiful Capital City.

BIRDSEYE VIEW OF "EL CAMINO CAPITAL" SHOWING PROPOSED STATE HIGHWAY FROM
SACRAMENTO THROUGH THE "NETHERLANDS OF AMERICA"

THE DELTA
OF THE SACRAMENTO
BY S.W. DOWNEY

RITING in *"Californian,"* February 6th, 1847, of Sacramento River and the time when "bright stars and stripes were first exhibited to the wondering savage," "Observer" says : "The broad bosom of its waters, which has for ages and ages 'known no sound, save its own dashing waters,' and been undisturbed, save by the solitary and frail rush canoe of the Indian, will, ere long, be whitened by the numerous sails, or darkened by the smoke of adventurous commerce."

Doubtless, Californians of the 40's smiled at the dreams of enthusiastic "Observer." Even to-day, when a record of splendid accomplishments has changed waste lands to fertile fields and transformed blighted tules into blooming orchards, Sacramento listens to naked facts, half incredulous, half skeptical. For, to Sacramento, as to the world, achievements of the "Delta" are wholly new and its unbounded possibilities but partly realized.

Quietly, but stubbornly, the River folk have faced their problems. No less pluckily, and just as surely as Dutch burghers reclaimed Holland, sturdy farmers of the Sacramento have driven back flood waters. To-day, the "Delta," "Land of California Nile," as it has been called by some, "Netherlands of America," as it has been called by others, is exuberant with life and beauty, a country in which to marvel and be glad.

HUGE DREDGERS HAVE MADE POSSIBLE THE RECLAMATION OF THOUSANDS OF FERTILE ACRES IN THE "SACRAMENTO DELTA"

Approximately 120,000 acres, reclaimed at an expenditure of $10,000,000.00, comprises the Sacramento "Delta"—probably the most productive district in the world. On its fertile land is grown asparagus, alfalfa, potatoes, onions, beans, barley, cantaloupes, peaches, pears, cherries, almonds, walnuts, and all manner of grain, garden produce, fruit and berries. Here is produced nearly one-fourth the asparagus of the United States. In 1911, Libby, McNeal & Libby, at their two canneries on Grand and Brannan Islands, canned 150,000 cases of this product, and 300,000 boxes were shipped in 1910. Two hundred and fifty bushels of potatoes to the acre are frequently raised, so many, that, says the river wit: "It is necessary to rent land on which to pile them." In the Lisbon District, one acre, planted with first year alfalfa seed, raised 10 tons, and 48 acres, similarly planted, grew 367 tons. During the same season, a thousand acre tract of barley yielded 42,000 sacks, averaging 110 pounds each, and sixty sacks have been produced on a single acre. In this luxuriant country are grown the world's earliest cherries—cherries, that last April, in New York City, sold for $100.00 a box. Here, also, are two acres, planted to cherries, that, this year, cleared $3,500.00, and 70 acres of orchard, that, in 1911, netted $43,024.13. Pear lands, throughout the district, pay more than $400.00 to the acre, and 40 per cent of California's entire Bartlett pear crop is produced in the general river territory south of Sacramento.

The United States Engineer's office in San Francisco shows that, in 1910, 382,000 tons of agricultural and horticultural produce were shipped from river lands of the "Delta" to Sacramento or Bay cities. Grain and hay shipments from the plains and hills, and freight, originating in either of

SACRAMENTO RIVER SCENE

the termini, are eliminated.   This vast tonnage, valued at the ridiculously low rate of 3 cents per pound, would be worth the enormous sum of $23,000,000.00.

The time others give to telling what land has produced, Delta people spend in ascertaining what theirs *can* produce.   They have not borne the heartache of reclamation struggle to "fling to the winds the golden grain."   Knowing that "spendthrift nation and spendthrift man, in the end, pay the same penalty and face the same law," they are solving problems of conservation, transportation, and fruit standardization, pests and blights   For flood control and navigation improvement everywhere along the river, they are battling with spirit invincible.   The California Debris Commission, made up of Army Engineers, has submitted to Congress a plan to improve navigation, reclaim 400,000 fertile acres and render absolutely secure 300,000 already reclaimed.   By foresight and industry, aided, maybe, by genius, inland towns abroad have been made seaports.   Who knows? As to-day sees the Sacramento a thoroughfare of local commerce, tomorrow may see flags of the nations upon its waters.

The latest, and not the least important, proposed project along the River, is that of constructing a highway, paralleling its east bank, from Sacramento, through the "Delta," and thence, by the most direct and practicable route, through Contra Costa and Alameda Counties, into Oakland. At the terminals lie two of the three state centers of population   Sacramento Valley and the Bay cities.   Between, is a region unexcelled for crop quantity and diversity, and of surpassing beauty.

OCHSNER BUILDING

Much grading, that would be required, has already been done. Road material abounds in the Contra Costa hills, and Reclamation districts have offered dredgers and assistance. To-day, the shortest passable route to the Bay cities, is by way of Stockton, 112 miles, while the road proposed, will be "75 miles, and a highway all the way."

The approaching Panama Pacific Exposition renders this road doubly desirable. What we can never hope to bring to the Exposition, we can bring the Exposition to see. If the "mountain cannot come to Mahomet, let Mahomet come to the mountain."

A state highway through the "Garden of the Netherlands" will bring homeseekers from every state in the Union and every country of the globe to the world's richest agricultural region, showing to them, within a radius of a few miles, acre after acre, each with a different yield.

"High cost of living" and "wasted wealth" go hand in hand. Europe, over good roads, transports for 9 cents what America, over bad roads, hauls for 23 cents. Every cent of the vast difference, totaling millions and millions of dollars, is waste. In proportion, therefore, as good roads traverse productive regions, wealth is conserved and cost of living reduced. Of inestimable importance,

THE H. S. CROCKER CO BUILDING

accordingly. is the construction from the $18,000,000.00 state highway fund, of a road through the "Delta"—a region unexcelled the world over for fertility and productiveness.

Under the name "El Camino Capital" (Highway of the Capital), the River Road is a link in the suggested "Pasear" of Panama-Pacific Expositicn. Two other roads, "El Camino Real" (Highway of the King), proceeding from San Francisco to Los Angeles, along the coast, and through old missions, and "El Camino Sierra" (Highway of the Sierras), running from Los Angeles north to Tahoe, along the east line of the beautiful Sierras, skirting Mt. Whitney, and connecting with branch road to Yosemite, complete the "Pasear"—destined to become world-famous, and designed to show the "sublimity of the ocean, the desolation of the desert, the grandeur of the mountains, and the opulence of the valley."

For years "Netherlands of America" has been inaccessable to strangers- even to Sacramento. True, people journey in steamboats down river, but levees thirty feet high, and higher, obscure the farms. Although the line of progress follows the course of highways, the "Delta," isolated as it is, has developed and waxed rich. With communication established, its future is limitless. "El Camino Capital," rising high above surrounding country will disclose from river to sky line green fields and incomparable orchards, and he who comes to temporize, will remain to build.

ROSE ARBOR, IN BLOOM   HOME OF MRS. WILLIAM BECKMAN

TUESDAY CLUB — IT'S HISTORY

BY MRS. WILLIAM BECKMAN

THE Tuesday Club of Sacramento was organized in 1896, and, at a meeting held in the parlors of Mrs. William Beckman, the writer was chosen as the Club's first president by the seventeen charter members. So much enthusiasm was manifest from its incipiency, that, within two months the membership had increased to more than fifty members, making it necessary to secure a hall for the meetings. Thus, from the nucleus of a small beginning, has evolved the Club of to-day, numbering six hundred, with its scope of usefulness and untiring energy.

From social reunions, musical programs, lecturers and miscellaneous subjects, the Club, in its fourth year, began its public work by sending a petition to the Board of City Trustees, requesting it to pass on an ordinance prohibiting the granting of any more saloon licenses in the residence portion of the city. The ordinance passed, and is still in effect.

The membership increased and became the recognized center of social and mental culture, and, with the purpose of encouraging all movements 'or the betterment of society, to further the education of women and foster a generous public spirit in the community, it was deemed wise to divide the large body into smaller departments in order to facilitate study along different lines to suit the diverse tastes of its members.

In the fifth year, work of a philanthropic nature was undertaken and proved a success in every respect. There was an ardent campaign, which resulted in carrying the High School Bonds; also,

NEW HOME OF THE TUESDAY CLUB

completing the work begun in the Club for the introduction of manual training in the schools. Through the Club's energies, domestic science is now taught in our schools. It gives liberally to the Traveler's Aid Society, and to all of a charitable nature the Club is foremost in helping, financially, within its powers, and, from its infancy, the members began to devise methods whereby our city would be improved, and, from the Club's department, came a recommendation to organize an Improvement Club. Favorable action was taken on this, and the result was that, with other women's organizations, the Women's Council was formed, which now numbers between 2,000 and 3,000 earnest, active women, whose object is for the betterment of this city and county along all lines.

In 1900, a committee from the Tuesday Club interviewed the city trustees, requesting the purchase of a park, containing about forty acres, to be preserved as a park for the use of the citizens and a playground for children. By energy, persistence and persuasion, with opposition from many, the committee finally won. The park, purchased for $12,500.00, and named McKinley Park, is now valued by the trustees at $100,000.00.

In 1902, the Club established three traveling libraries, being the second in the State to send these traveling bits of sunshine and knowledge to those living in remote districts. They were greatly appreciated, and proved a blessing to those who were away from circulating libraries.

In 1903, the Club, with the idea of owning its own club house, formed a corporation from among its members, calling it the "Tuesday Club House Association," to which the Club donated $300.00, as a nucleus for a club house fund. Since then, the aim and energy of the association has been bent toward securing funds to build a house, suitable for the housing of the progressive Tuesday Club—

NEW POWER PLANT OF THE GREAT WESTERN POWER COMPANY IN THE SIERRAS

one that would be a credit to the city and the women who have worked so tirelessly for the better-ment of their homes and their city, and now they feel that the romance of action, full of pulsing life and strong endeavor, has repaid them—in the fullest, in the mingling of personalities, in the culmin-ation of hopes, fruition, purposes and work, for one great object has been accomplished, and, in a few months, the Club will be housed within a $30,000.00 building, which will ever be a monument to the indomitable will and energy of the earnest workers who have labored for the good of one and all.

In thought, energy and achievement the Club women have not spared themselves in any useful work, but have felt they were not called into time to curl up in our hollow shells, but are here for a purpose, and are working for the common welfare, knowing there are vast social movements evinced everywhere. To-day does not know to-morrow, yet we feel that our efforts to build and fortify the virtue of the world will build and fortify our own.

We are not content to sit in the valley of the shadow of ignorance and idleness, but find time to shake the dust from our brains and clothes and strive to help, even while we are being helped, know-ing that the survival of the fittest must give way to the fitting of all to survive. A nation rises no higher than the life of the women comprising it, and our State, being the fairest in the diadem of the cluster, and our own city, its capital, we, of the Club feel, that in unity there is strength, and, with the advent of a new age of growth, increased liberality of sentiment, and a definite action concerning the welfare of the community, we of the six hundred—officers and members alike—are banded together to do something to lift the shadows of ignorance and errors, knowing that as we toil and work in the field of progression, we are broadening the way and making steps for those who come after us.

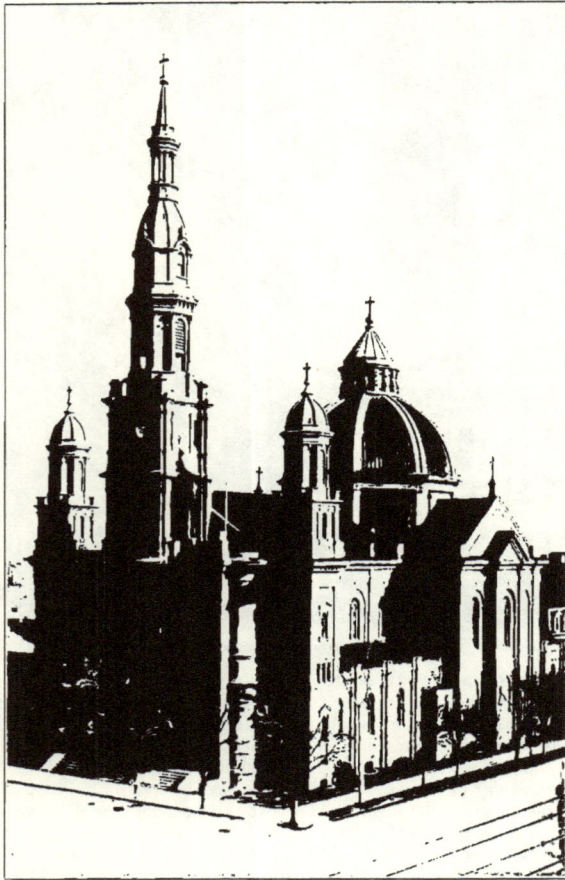

CATHEDRAL OF THE BLESSED SACRAMENT

SACRAMENTO'S SCHOOLS & CHURCHES

BY RT. REV. Wᴹ HALL MORELAND, D.D.

THE story of Sacramento's progress would be incomplete without reference to the abundant provision made for the intellectual and spiritual growth of the people. Beginning with tiny tots of four years old in excellent kindergartens, the public school system carries the boys and girls through a scientific process of mental discipline and training which fits them for active life or the university. There are twenty-two school buildings in the city, two hundred and fifty teachers employed, and eight thousand pupils in attendance. In addition to the common branches, children of the elementary schools are instructed in manual training, cooking and domestic arts. A school for the deaf is maintained where mutes are taught to use and understand the oral language. An elementary evening school, with ten teachers, is provided, and, also, a night high school. The city is justly proud of its new High School, its superior faculty, its fine grade of scholarship, and the splendid equipment of the building and grounds. Ten years ago the High School had but two hundred and eighty pupils. At this time the enrollment is about nine hundred. In fact, the pressure upon the present building is so great that the Board of Education is now considering another building within an area of from ten to twenty acres on the eastern side of the city, where, in addition to advanced work, agriculture may be taught. In 1911 the voters, at a special election, set aside $800,000 for the extension of public school advantages within the city. The most important feature in education is the personality of

HIGH SCHOOL BUILDING

the teacher. Sacramento's teachers are a body of high-minded, progressive, unselfish men and women. Their earnest lives and Christian character are unconsciously telling upon the future of the pupils entrusted to their charge. The Superintendent of Schools, the Board of Education, and other officials are men respected in the community for ability and public service.

Even more important than the schools, are the churches to the life of Sacramento. The solid foundation of real Christianity is the basis of our civilization. The fountain head of public spirit, unselfishness, commercial honesty, cleanness of life, domestic happiness and brotherly love is to be found in the constant preaching and practice of these virtues among the Christian people of the community. The churches are silently generating an atmosphere of high-mindedness, responsibility to God and one's fellows, and every beautiful and spiritual demand upon character, without which the whole community would sink to sordid and material ideals.

All the important churches are represented. The Roman Catholic Church and the American Episcopal Church maintain their Bishop and other chief ministers at Sacramento, which is the center of operations for these great and well-organized churches throughout the northern part of California. The Cathedral of the Blessed Sacrament is an imposing building, whose spire rivals in height the dome of the State Capitol. The Episcopal Church has secured a full half block in the best residence section upon which it has erected a Bishop's residence and Cathedral house, preparing for the future, when the temporary wooden structure, now used as a Pro-Cathedral, will be replaced by a Cathedral Church. St. Francis' Roman Catholic Church, St. Paul's Episcopal Church, which is built of granite, Westminster Presbyterian Church, which is of brick, are recent structures which would be a credit

INTERIOR SECTION OF CROCKER ART GALLERY, LARGEST COLLECTION
OF FAMOUS PAINTINGS IN THE WEST

to any city. There are also excellent churches of the following denominations: Methodist, Methodist South, Baptist, Christian or Disciples, Lutheran, both English and German, Evangelical, United Brethren. There is a synagogue largely attended by the Hebrew population, which constitutes one of the most valued and respected elements in the community. The Christian Scientists have lately erected an edifice. The Sacramento City Mission is a powerful agency for the relief of the poor, and is conducted by a board of directors on which sit Jews and Christians of every name. The City Mission conducts a Day Nursery, where working women can leave their children, and, during the canning season, this Nursery takes care of over one thousand children monthly. It also carries on an Emergency Home, Shelter for Homeless Men, Relief Store, Wood Yard and free Employment agencies for men and women. The efficient co-operation of the religious bodies of the community in the work of the City Mission is the best evidence of the fraternal spirit which unites Hebrews and Christians in a common cause. The city abounds in established works and institutions of mercy, such as orphanages, rescue homes, hospitals, the Home of the Merciful Saviour for Invalid Children (which ministers to helpless little ones in all the northern counties); and the charitable spirit of the community generously sustains these institutions with increasing abundance. To sum up this review of spiritual conditions in Sacramento, we may say without exaggeration, that no earnest, religious settler of any Christian persuasion whatever will fail to find opportunity for the practice of his religious faith and the training of his children in the church of his choice. He will also find a community in which religion is deeply respected, and its essential character recognized.

HOME OF HARRY THORP, ORANGEVALE

SACRAMENTO HOMES

BY MORRIS BROOKE

SACRAMENTO, the capital of the great State of California, offers much of the substantialities and pleasures of life, not only to those who seek to acquire wealth, but to such as desire an ideal residential city, where nature and art combine to insure the most happy results.

Here, midst the wealth of foliage, flowers, fruit and genial salubrious clime, a real home among cultured, sociable neighbors is available for the man of moderate, as well as of ample means.

A large portion of the residences are owned by those who occupy them, this being due, both to a high degree of prosperity and to those natural and other advantages which commend the city as a place in which to live. The agreeable climate largely accounts for this condition. People who have traveled all the way to the health resorts of Southern Europe declare, that but in few places, have they found conditions more inviting to the health seeker than in Sacramento and vicinity. The records of the weather bureau show the following figures for a period covering thirty-five years:

Average winter temperature,	48 degrees	Average summer temperature,	75 degrees
Average fall temperature,	61 degrees	Average highest temperature,	100 degrees
Average lowest temperature,	29 degrees	Mean of summer maxima,	87 degrees
	Mean of summer minima,	58 degrees	

RESIDENCE OF D. W. CARMICHAEL

In the midsummer months, when people throughout the East are sweltering from the heat, and horses are dropping in the street, nobody suffers in Sacramento. The evenings are always cool, and blankets are required. The winter months are much milder than in eastern and northern states, and, while here and there a heavy frost falls, it cannot be said that the temperature is disagreeable. The records of the local and state boards of health show the monthly mortality of Sacramento to be generally the lowest in the State.

The width of the lots, ranging from forty to eighty feet or more, and their reasonable price are desirable features. Thus, ample opportunity is afforded for growing ornamental shrubbery, fruit and flowers of practically all semi-tropical varieties. Here the camellia flourishes in all its beauty, producing waxen flowers of various hues. At Christmas time violets and pansies begin to bloom. During March the ever-plentiful and luxuriant calla lily bursts forth in its chaste beauty. Geraniums are in flower at all times, and during the greater part of the year roses of many varieties beautify the surroundings.

The style of architecture among the residences is varied. Among the stately mansions may be found artistic bungalows and cozy cottages, each vieing with the other in attractiveness. The unique California bungalow, so often spoken of, is quite popular in the newer and suburban sections. A pleasing feature in the construction of these is the use of hard cobble stones for pillars, foundations and chimneys. These stones are very plentiful in and about the American River bed some ten miles from Sacramento. Along the banks of this historic river, in the vicinity of Fair Oaks, are the most

beautiful orange, lemon and olive groves in the world. It is here where some of the prettiest suburban homes are found, homes that Easterners have often dreamed of and here have found their dreams come true.

While bungalows are quaint and pretty, yet many prefer the full two and three story residences. One would but have to take an automobile trip around the state capitol, then out into the suburbs to obtain an idea as to the many nice homes. A student of architecture could learn much, and could obtain many new ideas from these typical California homes. Brick is used but sparingly, owing to the mildness of the climate.

It has often been said that Sacramento is a city of homes. To the writer's knowledge, parties from the East, and even from our western metropolis, San Francisco, whose destiny, like our own, could not be brighter, have commented on the prettiness of the Sacramento homes. These favorable comments are but natural, coming from people who have, for the most part, been subject to the crowded life of larger cities.

The Panama-Pacific International Exposition in 1915, is now but three years away, a fair which will startle the whole world with its magnificence and grandeur. The people of Sacramento only desire to develop their untold resources, build better and prettier homes, and beautify their city in every possible way and in this manner help prepare for that notable occasion. For it can well be said that California is a great state, and, as time rolls on, the beautiful California of to-day will be but a pleasing recollection to the California of to-morrow.

ALONG THE BANKS OF THE SACRAMENTO

www.ingramcontent.com/pod-product-compliance
Lightning Source LLC
Chambersburg PA
CBHW032121080426
42733CB00008B/1004